* (LITERALLY "MANY FORMS") ONE WHO SPECIALISES IN THE ART OF DISGUISE

THE WASHERMAN AND THE POTTER

THE WASHERMAN AND THE POTTER

THE ANSWER IS NO

THE WISE ANSWER

BIRBAL THE WITTY
TALES OF BIRBAL

The route to your roots

BIRBAL THE WITTY

Birbal's fame had spread far and wide. As Akbar's favourite minister, he had an answer to every question and a solution to every problem. In fair tribute to his shrewdness, even the mighty Shah of Persia addressed Birbal as the 'Ocean of Intelligence'. Combining tact and common sense with a fair pinch of humour, he won his master's heart.

Script
Kamala Chandrakant

Illustrations
Ram Waeerkar

Editor
Anant Pai

Cover illustration by: C.M. Vitankar

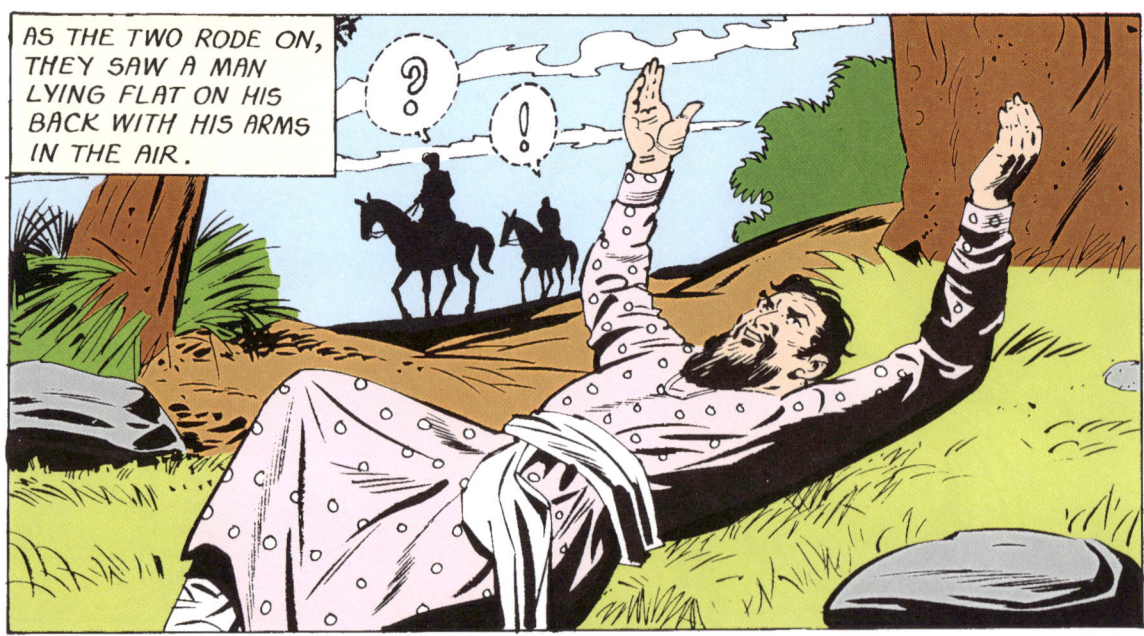

*MUSLIM PRIEST †COINS

AMAR CHITRA KATHA

3-IN-1

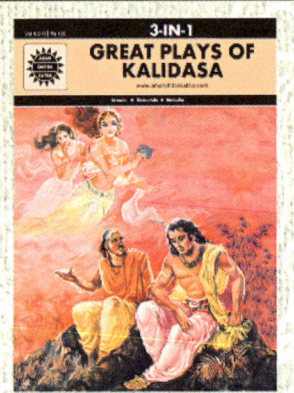
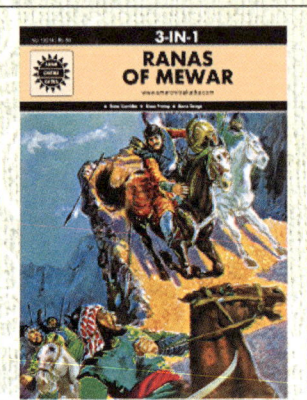

Over 50 titles available in paperback

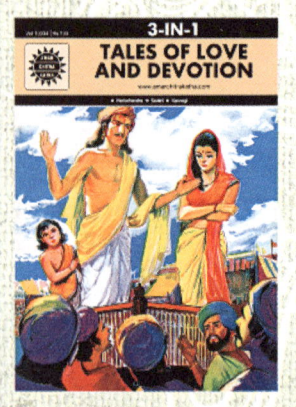

All titles available on www.amarchitrakatha.com

BIRBAL THE JUST

TALES OF BIRBAL

The route to your roots

BIRBAL THE JUST

Rogues and scoundrels were forced to tread carefully – even the exalted emperor was not spared when he erred – for Birbal, Akbar's able minister, was at hand to dispense justice. Part detective, part psychologist, he never failed to nab a wrongdoer. His methods might have been unorthodox – he once summoned a tree as the key witness in a case – but he never failed to get the desired results.

Script	Illustrations	Editor
Anant Pai	A.S. Chitrak	Anant Pai

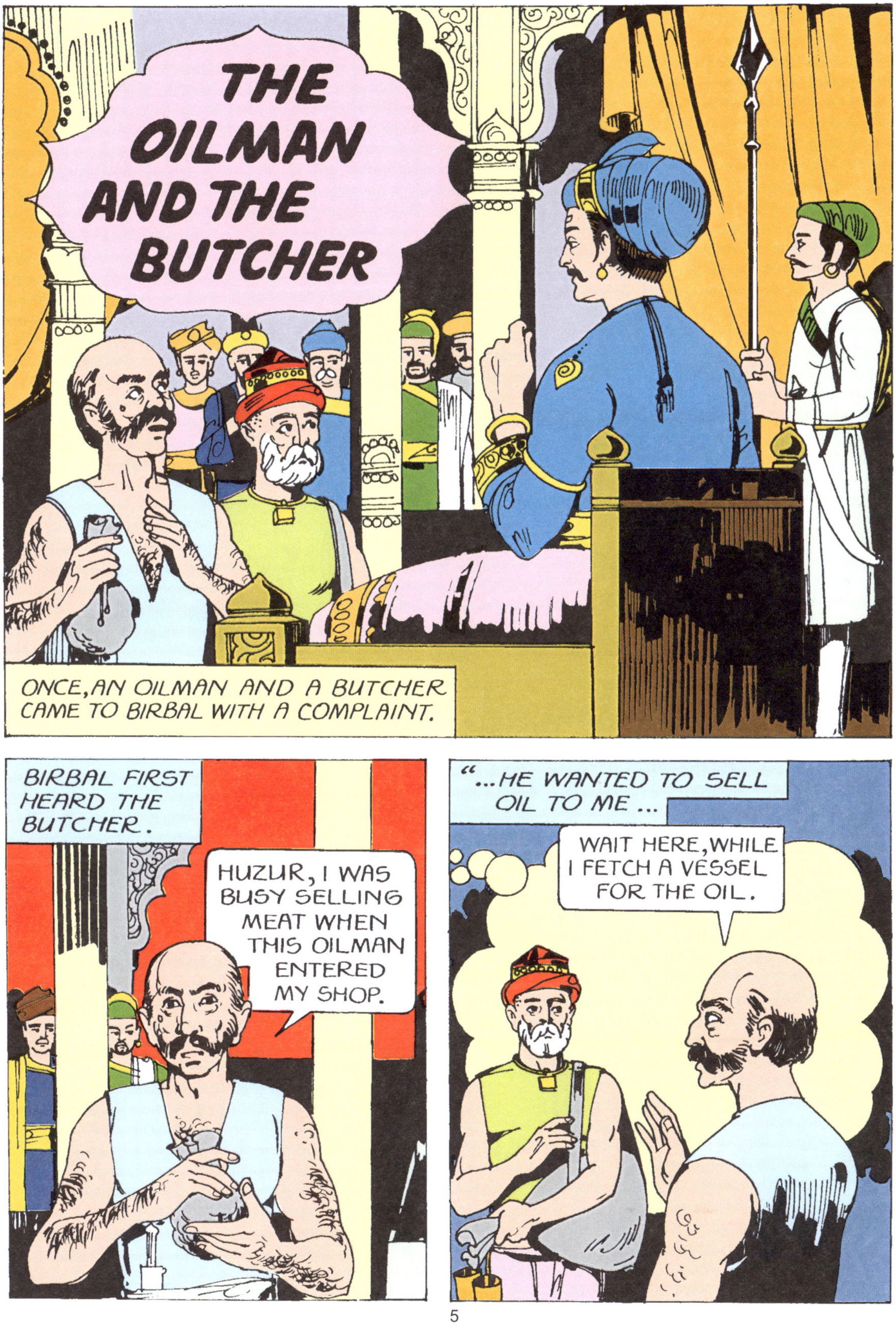

THE OILMAN AND THE BUTCHER

Once, an oilman and a butcher came to Birbal with a complaint.

Birbal first heard the butcher.

"Huzur, I was busy selling meat when this oilman entered my shop."

"...He wanted to sell oil to me...

Wait here, while I fetch a vessel for the oil."

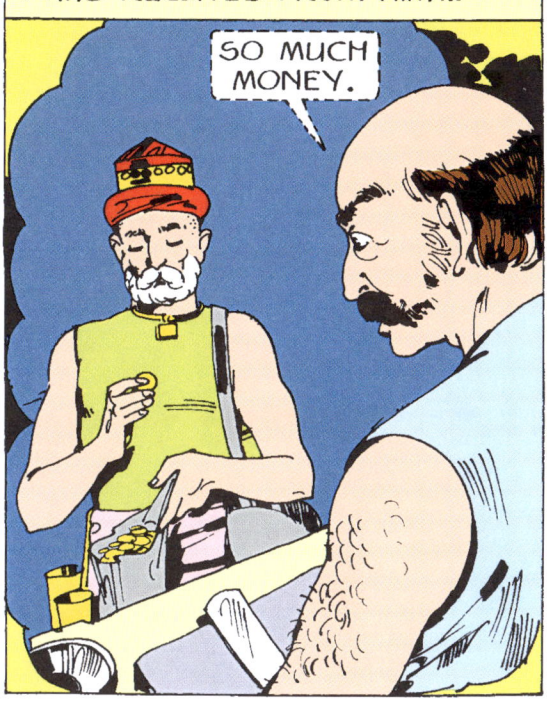

THE RELIABLE WITNESS

AN OLD MAN WENT ON A PILGRIMAGE AFTER GIVING A BAG CONTAINING A THOUSAND GOLD COINS TO HIS FRIEND FOR SAFE-KEEPING.

WHEN HE RETURNED —

FRIEND, I AM BACK HOME. PLEASE RETURN MY BAG.

WHAT BAG ARE YOU TALKING ABOUT? YOU NEVER GAVE ME ANY.

THE BAG CONTAINED ALL MY SAVINGS. PLEASE DON'T JOKE WITH ME. GIVE ME MY BAG.

WHAT BAG ARE YOU TALKING ABOUT? YOU NEVER GAVE ME ANY, YOU OLD FOOL.

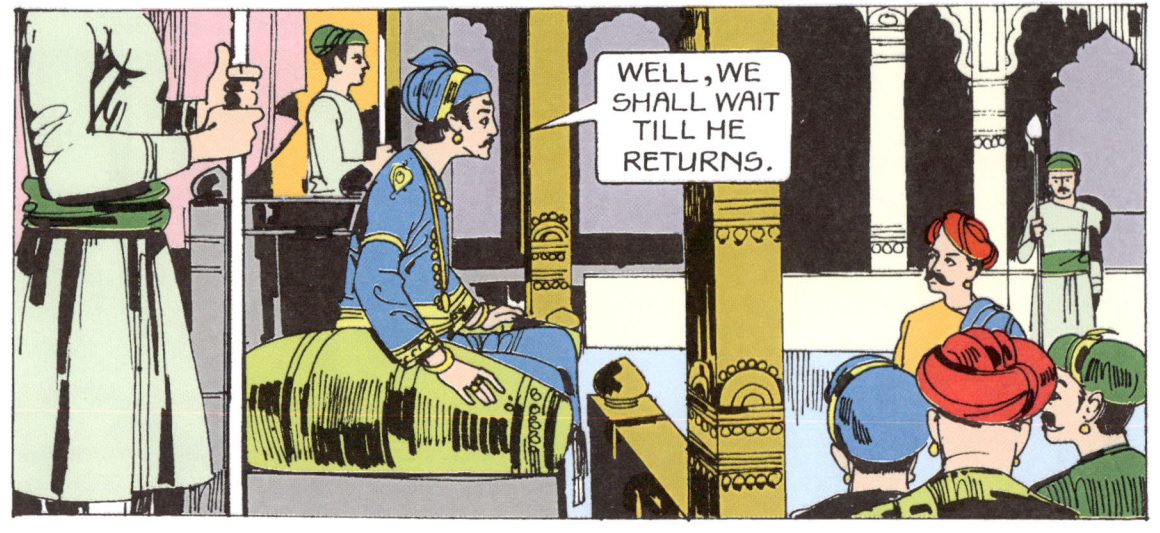

BIRBAL'S KHICHDI*

ONCE, DURING WINTER, AKBAR, BIRBAL AND A FEW COURTIERS STOPPED FOR A WHILE NEAR A LAKE, A COUPLE OF MILES AWAY FROM THE PALACE.

AS AKBAR STEPPED INTO THE ICE-COLD LAKE TO WASH HIS HANDS AND FEET, AN IDEA STRUCK HIM.

ANYONE, WHO CAN STAND IN THIS ICE-COLD WATER UPTO HIS NECK FOR ONE WHOLE NIGHT, WILL RECEIVE 50,000 GOLD COINS FROM ME.

* A DISH PREPARED OUT OF RICE AND LENTILS.

THE WICKED KAZI

IN THE DAYS OF AKBAR, THE PEOPLE HAD RESPECT FOR KAZIS, FOR THEY WERE THE OFFICIALS APPOINTED BY THE EMPEROR TO SETTLE DISPUTES. BUT THE KAZI OF DELHI WAS A DISHONEST MAN.

ONE DAY, A POOR WOMAN CAME TO HIM.

SIR, PLEASE KEEP THIS BAG IN YOUR CUSTODY TILL I RETURN FROM MY PILGRIMAGE. IT CONTAINS A THOUSAND GOLD COINS.

HAVE YOU SEALED THE BAG?

YES, I HAVE.

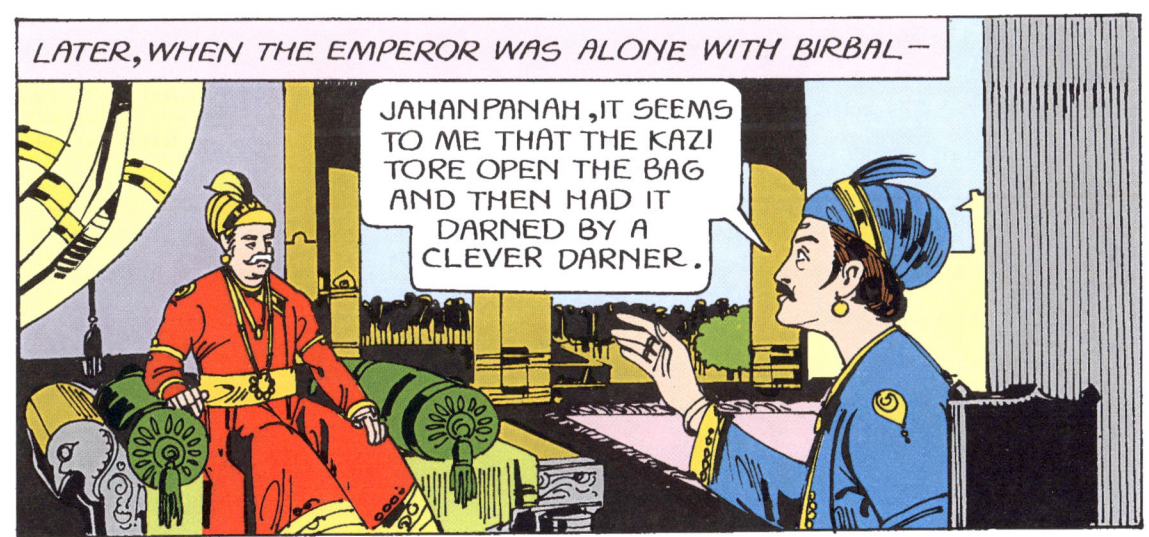

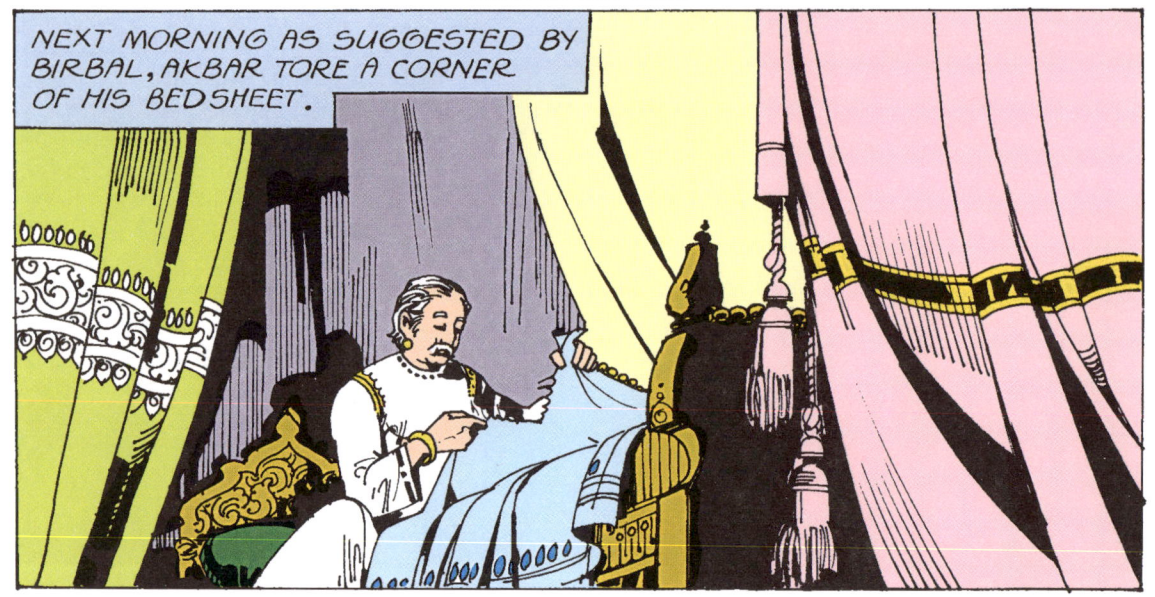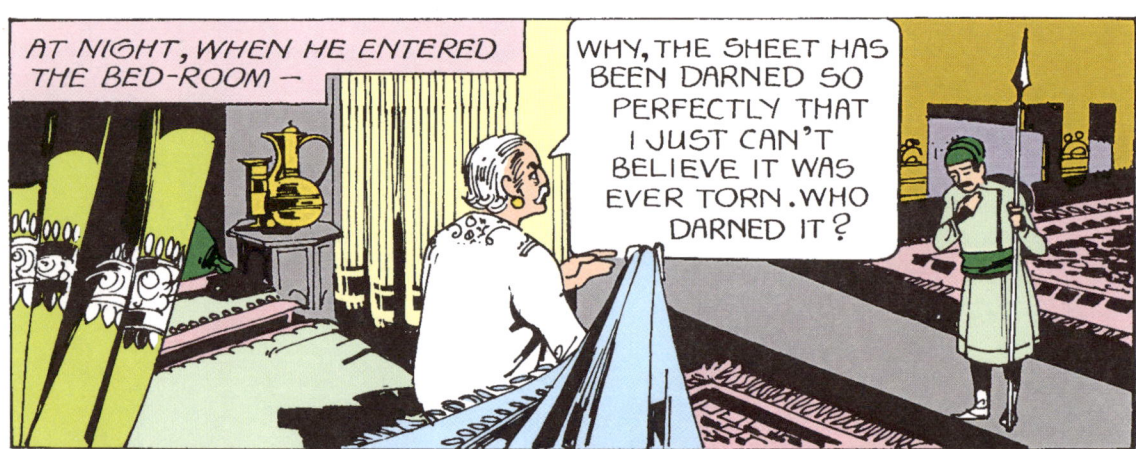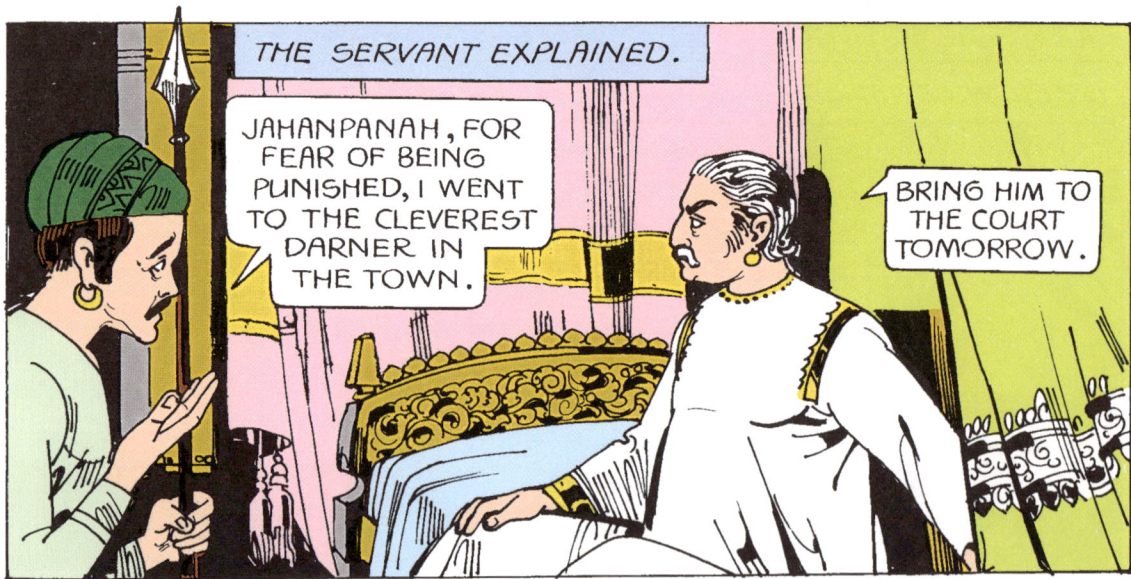